In the In-Between

A Story of Almosts and Maybes

Puneet Gill

The Publisher and Editor shall not be liable whatsoever...

Made with ♥ on the BookLeaf Publishing Platform
www.bookleafpub.in
www.bookleafpub.com

To the love that nearly was,

To the whispers left unheard,

To the love that was felt yet never returned.

And to myself— for embracing the ache, finding
beauty in the in-between, and daring to feel it all.

Acknowledgement

This book would not exist without the people and emotions that shaped it.

To the one who made me feel everything—this journey was both breathtaking and heartbreaking. Though you may never read this, you will always exist in the spaces between these words.

To the people who stood by me, listened without judgment, and let me be my raw, unfiltered self— you know who you are. Your kindness is a treasure.

And finally, to myself—for turning pain into poetry, for daring to bleed onto these pages, for proving that even in the in-between, my voice holds worth and unfinished stories deserve to be told.

To every reader holding this book— Thank you for stepping into this space. You are seen. You are felt. You are not alone.

Preface

Life has a way of placing us in moments suspended between clarity and chaos, between love and loneliness, between holding on and letting go. This book is born from that space— the in-between.

These poems are fragments of a heart that loved fiercely, a soul that felt too deeply, and a voice that once trembled but now speaks. They hold the words I never got to say, the emotions I never knew how to unravel, and the truths I had to face alone.

If you've ever found yourself lost in the undefined—lingering between the past and the future, questioning whether love was real even when it was never truly yours—this book is for you. May you find pieces of your own story within these pages.

In the In-Between

I exist in the pause between heartbeats,
where love is felt but never declared.
Where your eyes hold promises,
that your lips will never attest.

I linger in the spaces between touches,
where fingertips graze but never stay.
Where every 'almost' feels like forever,
yet fades like echoes drifting away.

I am caught between yesterday and
tomorrow,
between holding on and letting go.
A love not lost, yet never found,

a story half-written in the margins of
"almost."

You stand on one side, I on the other,
bridged only by words left unspoken.
Between presence and absence,
between yearning and silence,
between what was and what will never be.

And so I stay—
not with you, not without you,
but somewhere in the in-between.

An Almost Forever

We almost had it, didn't we?
A love oscillating between the unsaid and the
undone,
written in whispers, erased by silence,
a story that never turned its page.

Hands that reached but never held,
palms aching for a touch that hovered, then
hesitated.
Fingers drawn close, only to tremble,
caught between yearning and restraint.

Words that danced on trembling lips,
fluttering like fragile birds in flight,
but caged by fear, swallowed whole,

never finding the courage to be felt.

We were a question left unanswered,
a song that faded mid-melody,
a flame that flickered in the dark,
but never grew into a fire.

And now, I walk through echoes of you,
through half-formed memories and aching
voids,
forever wondering—
what might have been,
had love dared to cross the in-between?

Half Goodbye

I have left you a thousand times,
in my mind, in my heart, in whispered
prayers.
Yet each morning, I wake still tangled,
in the places where you belong.

I tell myself this isn't real—
not fully, not the way it should have been.
But love does not ask for permission,
nor does it vanish when left unanswered.

I say goodbye in fragments,
in unread messages and unshed tears,
in the way I search for you in strangers,
or pause at the echo of familiar songs.

I walk forward, but never alone,
for you are the shadow trailing my steps.
A love unfinished, a door left ajar,
a farewell never fully spoken.

And so I go, not with you, not without you,
but somewhere in between—
always leaving, never gone.

Ephemeral Us

We are a story written in passing,
held together by borrowed time.
A fire that burns bright in the dark,
but never belongs to the dawn.

A touch that lingers, yet fades to dust,
like echoes swallowed by the morning air.
Fingers tracing eternity in seconds,
Only to slip into the spaces between.

We live in glances, in fleeting nights,
in words too fragile to stay.
Not a love to last, nor one to forget,
but one that hums beneath my skin.

A presence felt in echoes, not in steps,
a heart held, yet weightless as dust.
No promises made, no endings carved—
just a love that exists, yet never stays.

Unforgotten, Yet Uncertain

You say I live in your every thought,
that my absence lingers like an ache.
You hear my name and feel me there,
a shadow pressed against your chest.

And yet, I wonder—will time erase me?
Will love alone be enough to make me stay?
I carry you like an echo that never fades,
but will you hold me the same way?

I trace our moments, cradle them close,
but memories are fragile things.
Will I remain—soft, unseen—
or slip away like whispers on the wind?

You miss me, you love me, I know—
but fear still lingers in my veins.
For even the brightest stars can fade,
and even the deepest love is lost to time.

You Are My Home

Not four walls, not a place on a map,
but the curve of your voice in the dark.
Not an address, not a key in my hand,
but the way your touch felt like belonging.

I was home in the quiet between your words,
in the way you knew me before I spoke.
You were the warmth, the safe return,
the only place my heart could rest.

And now, I wander through rooms that do
not hold me,
wear a life that no longer fits.
Homeless—not in the world, but within,
adrift in the absence of you.

What I Never Said

The words sit heavy on my tongue,
too late, too lost, too much.
I shape them in the quiet dark,
but they wither before they touch the air.

I reach for you in unspoken ways,
in glances held too long, in half-drawn
breaths.
I wait for echoes, for something returned,
but silence lingers where answers should be.

I pour my heart into spaces between us,
into gaps you never see.
You take my love like light through glass—
felt, but never held.

And so, I gather the words I never said,
stack them like stones inside my chest.
They weigh me down, yet tether me close to
you,
the only proof that I once reached for you.

Crowded And Empty

Laughter swells, voices rise,
the world hums with life around me.
I nod, I smile, I play along,
but the quiet within me never fades.

I am here, yet somehow missing,
a ghost within my own skin.
Surrounded, yet untouched—
a presence unnoticed, a heart unheard.

The void hums beneath my ribs,
a silence that no noise can fill.
I reach, I speak, I exist--
but no one sees the hollow in my hands.

Holding Onto Nothing

I could let go, I could move on,
set the past adrift, let the echoes fade.
But who am I without this ache—
without the weight of what was almost mine?

The emptiness still fits me well,
a hollow carved in the shape of your name.
If I release the sorrow,
do I erase the proof that you were here?

Healing feels like quiet betrayal,
as if forgetting you means forgetting love.
So I hold on—not to you, not to us,
but to the ache that still feels like home.

In Another Life

In another life, your hand is in mine,
without hesitation, without fear.
No stolen moments, no careful distance—
just love, unshaken, unbound, ours.

There are no glances laced with longing,
no words swallowed to keep the peace.
Here, you love me in the open,
without shadows, without shame.

I do not wonder where I stand,
do not measure your love in half-spoken
truths.
You stay— not as a fleeting presence,
but as certainty, as home.

In another life, we do not ache,
do not break beneath the weight of almost.
We are not a question, a what-if, a someday—
we are everything, we are now.

When You Love Me

For once, I do not question—
not the touch, not the words,
not the way your eyes hold me
as if I have always belonged.

For once, I do not brace for distance,
for silence to swallow your warmth.
Your love does not arrive in halves,
but whole, unwavering, mine.

I live in the certainty of us,
in a world where you do not hesitate.
Where I am not an almost, a secret,
but the only answer you ever need.

Halfway To Nowhere

We walk the line between love and loss,
never daring to stray too far.
Fingers graze but never grasp,
hearts whisper, yet never say enough.

I call this love, but not out loud,
afraid the words will break the spell.
Afraid to lose the little I have,
even if it's never been mine to keep.

You pull me close, then disappear,
a rhythm I have learned by heart.
A dance of wanting, never having,
a road that leads to nowhere at all.

Loving In Grey

We are not bound, yet never free,
a love that floats, untethered, unseen.
No walls to hold us, no chains to break,
just a quiet longing we dare not name.

You reach for me, but never stay,
I hold you close, but never claim.
We move like shadows in borrowed light,
always near, never quite right.

And still, I find comfort here—
in the space between hello and goodbye.
Not whole, not lost, just something fleeting,
ephemeral, aching, and impossibly ours.

The Tide Between Us

You come like the ocean at dawn,
soft waves brushing against my shore,
a whisper of warmth, a sensational touch—
before the pull drags you away once more.

I stand where you leave me, waiting,
watching the ripples of where you were.
I swear I won't wade in again,
Yet the moment you return, I drown.

You never stay, but never leave,
always close enough to reach, yet
untouchable.
And still, I let you pull me under,
because even borrowed love feels real.

A Love That Wants More for Me

You hold my heart with careful hands,
never too tightly, never for too long.
You stand at the edge of us,
neither moving closer nor stepping away,
a presence felt but never claimed.

You tell me I deserve the sun,
though you can only offer the moon.
You trace constellations across my sky,
but remind me, with quiet sorrow,
that I need more than borrowed light.

You whisper, *Go where love can stay*,
though I see the ache in your gaze.
You choose my happiness over your heart,
even as yours shatters in the letting go.

And I wonder—
is there anything more selfless,
more beautiful,
than a love that loves me enough to wish me
away?

The Gift of My Absence

I stepped away so you could stand,
no longer waiting in my shadow.
I loved you enough to leave,
so you could find a love that stays.

No more half-promises, no quiet ache,
no longing for a future I can't give.
I let you go, not out of indifference,
but because you deserve certainty.

Without me, your world will bloom,
unburdened by the weight of almost-love.
And though I loved you in silence,
My absence is the loudest gift I could give.

A love that sets you free.

— Him.

Parallel Lives

We wake beneath different skies,
walk through different days,
but the same weight lingers in our chests,
a love neither of us dares to name.

We smile where we must,
carry on where we should,
but in the quiet, we exist in the same silence,
whispering to a love that only we can hear.

The world moves forward,
but we stand, side by side,
each carrying the pieces of a bond
we can't fully touch, but can never let go.

You walk your path, I walk mine,
but every step is laced with the same ache,
the same pull,
the unspoken truth that we are still here,
even when we cannot be.

And when the night falls,
when we are alone in our separate spaces,
we both feel it—
the bond we can't break,
the love we can't let go.

In Your Eyes, In Your Voice

In your eyes, I see oceans—
depths of unspoken words,
a thousand stories untold,
each glance a novel of its own.

Your voice is a melody,
soft as rain, fierce as wind,
every word a gentle reassurance,
every pause a prayer.

In the way you listen,
so patiently, so deeply,
I find the reflection of everything

I've ever longed to feel.

Your empathy is a river—
steady, quiet, and ever-flowing,
lifting the weight of those around you
without seeking anything in return.

And in your dedication,
I see the strength of mountains,
unwavering, patient,
refuge for all you hold close.

You are a harmony of grace and resilience—
a rare melody that plays only for those who
truly listen.

Illogical Emotions

My heart is a storm, wild and untamed,
a symphony of longing, yearning, and need.
Yet the world around me insists on calm,
a quiet order, a steady rhythm,
as if feeling too much were a crime.

I carry the weight of dreams,
unruly, sprawling like vines—
yet logic tells me to prune,
to tidy the mess of unspoken desires,
to fit them into neat, manageable lines.

My emotions surge like waves—
chaotic, unpredictable, relentless,
but practicality demands stillness,

urging me to stand firm
on dry, solid ground,
when all I want is to drift.

There is a battle between what I feel
and what I am supposed to do.
One pulls me into the depths of passion,
while the other tugs me back to reason—
a tug-of-war that leaves me divided,
suspended in a space
where both worlds collide.

And so I stand, trapped between
what my heart says and what my mind
demands,
lost in the complexity of emotions
that refuse to be caged
in the boxes life tries to build.

Unworthy

I whisper to myself in the hush of night,
that love was never meant for someone like
me.
I'm too flawed, too broken,
too tangled in the web of my own self-doubt
to be worthy of eternal affection.
A heart too bruised,
a soul too scarred—
perhaps love is not a thing
I was ever meant to hold.

I watch others wrapped in warmth,
hands held, hearts entwined,
and I wonder what it's like
to be chosen without question.

But I am not that person.
I am the one left standing,
watching from the shadows,
believing love is a privilege
I'll never be allowed to know.

I tell myself I don't deserve it,
that I am not enough
for the kind of love that stays,
that builds instead of breaks.
How could someone love me
when I can't even accept myself?

And yet, in the silence,
a part of me still longs
for what I claim I cannot have.
Perhaps I'm afraid to be seen,
to be loved,
because it might prove
what I've always feared—
that I am unworthy.

Bare

I stand here, bare,
stripped of armour,
of masks, of the walls
I built to barricade my heart.
In this space,
I am exposed—
not fragile,
but unguarded,
and it terrifies me.

I was always taught
to conceal the cracks,
to mend the fractures
with smiles and silence,

to pretend I am whole
when the truth is,
I am a mosaic of scars,
pieces scattered,
but still, I exist.

I wonder if you'll see me
as I truly am—
not a perfect picture,
but a reflection of every tear,
every fear,
every moment I allowed myself
to feel too deeply.
A fragile truth,
hanging in the balance
between trust and doubt.

But vulnerability is not weakness,
it's a strength I haven't learned to wield.
It's the courage to stand in the light
without masking the shadows,
to say, "I am here,
and I am enough,"
even when my heart quivers.

So I open myself to you,
knowing that you may see the cracks,
the jagged edges of my soul,
and yet, I offer them freely,
because this is who I am—
imperfect, raw,
and unafraid to be seen.

What the Moon Meant to Say

My glow is a secret—
a poem unfolding in phases,
a language of waiting, of wanting.
I am luminous yet unread,
spilling light in whispers, in stolen breaths.
My eyes hold untold stories,
my heart drifts between two different worlds.
Like the moon, I pull at unseen tides—
rising, receding—
a quiet enigma against the night.

Fragments of an Unfinished Thought

I gather myself in pieces,
a mosaic of half-truths and hesitation.
My thoughts are ink in water—
forming, unforming, dissolving.
I speak in ellipses,
never a beginning, never an end—
only the space between questions,
a pause waiting to belong.

Gravity of the Unsaid

Some words are meant to be spoken,
but they sink instead—
heavy as stones in a breathless river,
vanishing before they reach the surface.
I feel them pressing against my ribs,
ghosts knocking from beneath my skin,
pushing their weight into the marrow,
curling like unanswered prayers in my chest.
I swallow their echoes,
but they orbit me still,
like planets chained to an absent sun—
silent, unseen.

Epilogues without Endings

Stories should have full stops,
yet some only dissolve into gloom,
half-spoken, half-written—
like a thought paused but never erased.
The last page waits, unread, unfinished,
its ink refusing to settle,
its meaning suspended in the space
between longing and letting go.
Some tales do not have closures;
they spill into tomorrows,
woven into moments
that refuse to turn to dust.
Life moves without consent,
dragging our unwritten endings along,
until one day, we, too,
become a sentence left hanging in mid-air.

The Threshold of Tomorrow

The door creaks open,
another day begins.
I stand—
on the edge of almost.
You are here,
but not in the way I need,
a presence I cannot touch,
a silence I cannot soothe.
I reach for something
that never quite reaches back,
fingers slipping through the space
between want and reality.
The hurt is gentle—
like a quiet hum,
not enough to scream,
but enough to break.

We are undefined,
unsaid,
but always there,
in the hollow between now and never.
I stand still,
waiting for a name,
a word,
a return that never comes.
Here, at the threshold,
I hold on—
to nothing,
to everything that never was.

The Language of Withering

I have learned to love like autumn—
to offer warmth in the hush of fading hues,
to hold beauty even in the act of letting go.
There is poetry in withering,
in the quiet surrender of leaves to the wind,
A final bloom before the fall.

How I Think He Loves Me

I think he loves me in the way his gaze lingers,
careful not to betray the truth in his eyes,
as if every glance is a thought left unsaid,
each moment weighed with the tension of
what cannot be.
I think he loves me in the quiet ways,
when his presence fills the space between us,
yet he keeps his distance,
respecting what cannot be crossed,
but offering more than mere proximity.
I think he loves me in the subtle gestures,
a touch that's almost there,
a word that hovers just beneath the surface,

and I wonder how much he holds back,
for reasons only he truly knows.
I think he loves me in the silence of his
restraint,
not in acts that would be noticed,
but in the small sacrifices he makes—
avoiding what he desires most
for the sake of what he must protect.
I think he loves me in the moments
when he can't say it,
but I feel it,
lingering in the air,
unspoken,
untouched.
And though I know he cannot love me
in the way I ache for,
I can't help but see it in the small,
unseen places he lets himself exist.
He loves me,
but never enough to break
the boundaries that keep him tied
to the life he cannot leave.

And I,
bound to a love I know will never be
returned,
carry it deeply, quietly,
Unable to let go.

Somewhere, I Still Exist

He tells me to go—
to build a life where love is simple,
Where hands reach for me without hesitation,
where I do not have to wonder
how much of myself I is safe to give.
He says there is someone
who will love me the way I deserve,
but he does not understand
that love is not a thing I choose,
it is a thing that happened to me,
without permission,
without an escape.
And so I sit with this—
this knowing, this ache,
this quiet catastrophe of being his in every
way

except the ways that matter.
Somewhere, in another life,
I am not just a passing thought,
not just a moment he has to bury.
Somewhere, we are not defined
by restraint, by quiet goodbyes,
by the weight of a love
that will never find a home.
But in this life,
I am the one left holding it all,
carrying the fire he will never let burn,
watching him stay but not say,
as if keeping his distance
is the only kindness he knows how to give.

The Forever Kind

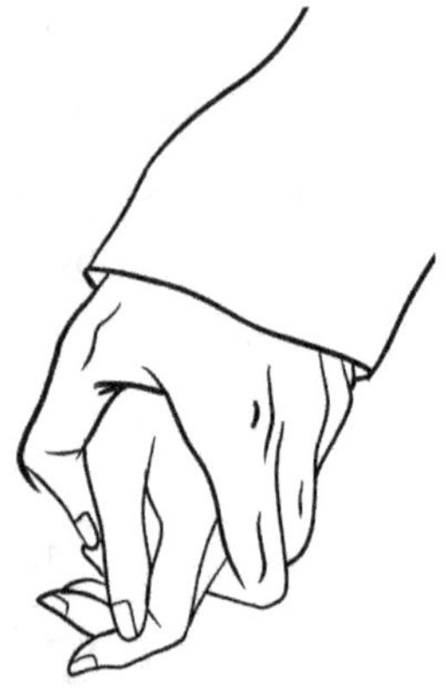

I do not know if love is meant to last,
if hearts are made to be given once,
or if they learn to belong again.
But I know this—
whatever I become,
wherever I go,
there will always be a part of me
that remains tethered to him.
Not in the way of waiting,
not in the way of hope,
but in the way the ocean belongs to the
moon—
pulled, restless, aching,
never free.

It terrifies me,
this knowing,
this quiet imprisonment of the heart.
To love once like this
and know I may never love again
With quite the same gravity.
And maybe that is its own kind of ending—
not the closing of a door,
but the acceptance
that some loves never leave.
They only settle deeper,
becoming part of the things
we carry but never name.

A Love like Prayer

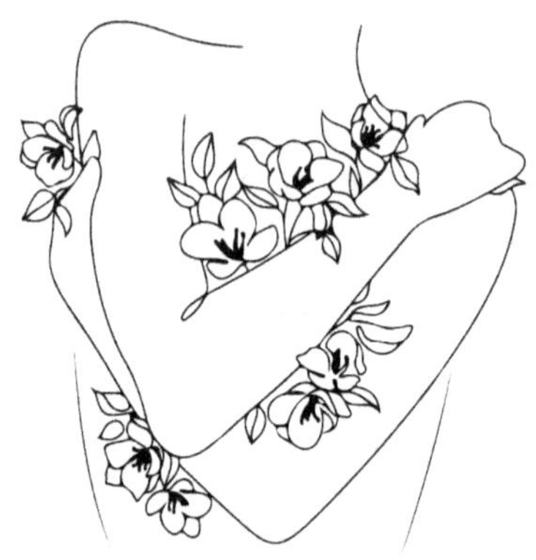

I do not ask for more than this—
to love him in the way the sun
loves the horizon,
knowing it will never hold the night,
yet reaching for it still.
I do not beg for answers,
only for the quiet mercy
of keeping him within me,
of letting this love exist
without permission,
without end.
He calls it love,
but love confined by edges,
by walls that do not bend,
by choices made long before me.

Yet still, it lingers between us,
a presence neither of us can name
without unravelling something deeper.
And so I do not fight it,
nor do I set it free.
I keep it close,
a quiet altar built in his name,
where hope and surrender kneel side by side.
And I pray—
but in shadows,
with every aching part of me,
offering this love to the only hands
that will ever know its weight,
asking—no, daring—
to be held.